CLOS _

the

DISTANCE

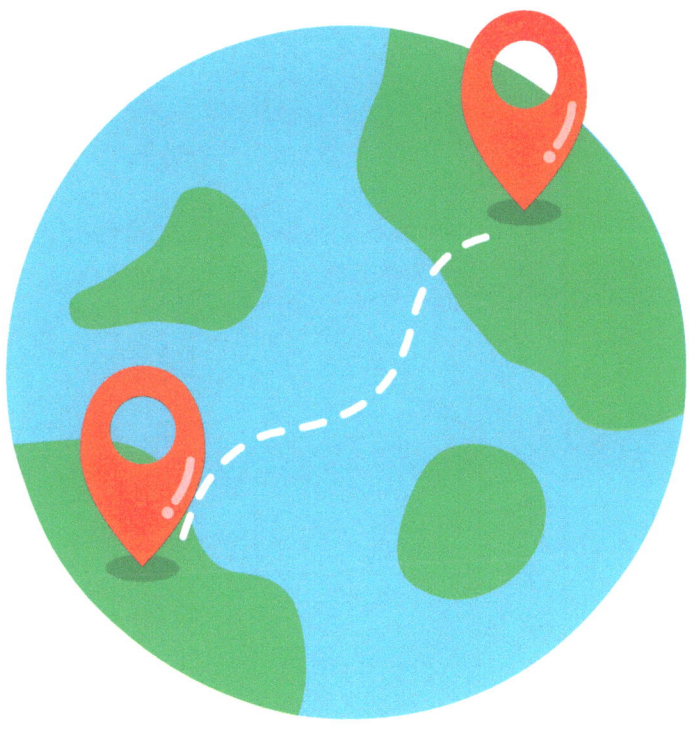

written by
Hannah Smart

Copyright © 2024 Hannah Smart.
All rights reserved.

Your year-long journey to long-distance fun, love and happiness starts here...

Your long-distance relationship offers unique opportunities for fun and creativity. This book provides you with 52 engaging tasks—one for each week of the year—that will bring you closer together, no matter how far apart you are. These tasks are carefully crafted to address various aspects of your relationship, ensuring balance and depth in your connection.

Getting Started

Pick a random number each week or open the book to a random page to discover your task for the week. The tasks are divided into eight categories, each serving a different purpose in your relationship.

Do you want to pick based on categories or available resources and time? No problem - head to the back of the book to see an index of tasks.

Completing these tasks will not only keep your relationship exciting and engaging but also help you navigate the ups and downs of long-distance love. Remember to use the tracker pages to mark off each completed task and celebrate your progress together.

Are you ready to embark on this year-long journey of connection, creativity, and love?
Let's get started and
Close the Distance.

PROGRESS TRACKER

- [ ] 1. Our Story in Photos
- [ ] 2. 7 Days of Us
- [ ] 3. Songs I Sing About You
- [ ] 4. Dinner for 1 + 1
- [ ] 5. It's So Unfunny, I Can't Stop Laughing
- [ ] 6. Mine & Theirs
- [ ] 7. Together Again
- [ ] 8. Steam & Bubbles
- [ ] 9. The 500 Mile Drive-In
- [ ] 10. Just Like Me... But Far Worse
- [ ] 11. Getting Date Ready
- [ ] 12. Start Your Day With Me
- [ ] 13. Just You, Me & the Great Outdoors
- [ ] 14. What Do You Meme?
- [ ] 15. Escape the Distance
- [ ] 16. The Moments I Miss You Most
- [ ] 17. The Book That Changed My Life...
- [ ] 18. Barry White Time

PROGRESS TRACKER

- [ ] 19. Before We Kick The Bucket
- [ ] 20. The Path That Led Me To You
- [ ] 21. 12 Months of Us
- [ ] 22. Right, Move Me Now... Or Later, Maybe
- [ ] 23. Real Snail Mail
- [ ] 24. Picture Post-Its
- [ ] 25. 7 Context-Free Days
- [ ] 26. Couples Who Play Together...
- [ ] 27. 7 Ways To Say I Love You
- [ ] 28. The Great Distance Bake Off
- [ ] 29. I Did Not Predict That!
- [ ] 30. Take Me Away
- [ ] 31. When We're Next Together
- [ ] 32. Relaxation Date
- [ ] 33. Legs Eleven
- [ ] 34. Wear Your Heart On Your Sleeve
- [ ] 35. The Fact of the Matter Is...

PROGRESS TRACKER

- [ ] 36. Me, You & Whatever You Want To Do
- [ ] 37. The Times It Got Hot
- [ ] 38. Happy Hamper
- [ ] 39. You're Pretty Handy
- [ ] 40. Sweet Dreams
- [ ] 41. Happily Ever After
- [ ] 42. Have You Heard?
- [ ] 43. Wish You Were Here
- [ ] 44. Places We'll Go, Things We'll See…
- [ ] 45. Monkey Hear, Monkey Do
- [ ] 46. You Time, On Me!
- [ ] 47. For Your Eyes Only
- [ ] 48. Things That Make Me Think Of You…
- [ ] 49. Healthy Prospects
- [ ] 50. Life Support Line
- [ ] 51. A Ditty or Two
- [ ] 52. When We're Apart…

thoughtful gifting
Our Story in Photos

Create a Relationship Collage

Create a collage of photos for your partner to hang on their wall. You have a few options for the execution of this task:

- Order prints of photographs and arrange them into a frame to ship to your partner
- Create a digital collage and order the print for delivery to your partner
- Create a digital collage to send via email/text

Some other ideas:

- If you don't have enough photos, find images online of places you have been, things you have done together and other meaningful images to create a visual memory board instead
- If you want to get super creative, create a video slideshow using software or an app and add a meaningful track as background music

Why?

When things get tough, few things will help to keep you more grounded and connected than remembering some of your best moments and achievements together.

TIP: Why not open together on the phone or video call to chat about the contents?

emotional connection
7 Days Of Us

Relationship Text Quiz

Answer a question a day, via text or call, or set aside time to go through all the questions together.

The questions:
1. What are your top 5 memories of me/us?
2. What is your favourite meal I cook/we go out for together?
3. What are your 5 favourite things about me?
4. What is it about us that you think makes us compatible?
5. What is your favourite way for us to spend time together?
6. Of all my friends and family, who do you like the most, and why?
7. Is there a place you have visited you'd love to take me to, and why?

Why?

The text quiz is about reminding each other what you love about each other. Trickle the questions across the week to answer as and when, or set aside a little time to run through the questions together to ensure you have an opportunity to bond and connect over each other's answers.

IDEA: Why not add in a few of your own questions for each other to answer?

closing the distance
Songs I Sing About You

Make a Playlist

Using your preferred music streaming service, create a playlist for your partner to listen to. If you need inspiration, you can use the prompts to help you pick.

Optional prompts:
- A song you don't know but I think you'd love
- A song with lyrics that make me think of us
- A song that reminds me of a time we were together
- A song that makes me feel happy
- A song I'd love to see live with you
- A song I can't listen to quietly
- A song to make you laugh

Why?

Most of us sing along to songs which make us think about our partner, whether it's simply because you know they like it or because the lyrics reflect part of your relationship. This task is about showing your partner what little things make you think about them throughout the day.

TIP: Remember to give a little explanation of why you added each song.

digital dating
Dinner for 1 + 1

Dinner Date!

Plan to cook and eat together whilst on a video call. If you're not a great chef, let your partner pick the recipe and guide you.

Make it more:
- Get dressed up for your dinner date and take selfies whilst getting ready
- Plan a surprise dinner by sending your partner for a click-and-collect supermarket order so they don't know what they're cooking until you are ready to tell them
- Go out or order in for a meal instead and chat whilst you eat

Why?

Eating together is a great time for couples to catch up, connect and feel close. Whilst that may seem impossible long-distance, with a little creativity, and some technology, anything is possible!

IDEA: Order matching boxes from a meal subscription service to make this last all week.

just for fun
It's so unfunny, I can't stop laughing

Joke of the Week

Send your partner a joke every day to see who gets the best laugh of the week!

Make it more:
- Set a theme each day for your jokes to make it trickier, or a theme for the week
- Send your joke as a video message so your partner can see you whilst you tell it to make it more connected
- Pick a joke with a little backwards and forwards and tell it over a video call
- Score each joke out of 10 and see what the overall scores are at the end of the week

Why?

Sometimes, the funniest jokes are the ones which actually weren't really funny at all! Laughing together is so important and often is overlooked when life and practicalities need to take priority. This week, taking 5 mins a day to make each other smile will be your priority.

IDEA: Why not share your jokes with friends/family and have them choose a winner for you?

the challenge cup
Mine & Theirs

My Partners Favorites Quiz

This spin on a popular hen-night game will put you both on the spot, and the winner shall be crowned the greatest fact retainer! Answer each of the following things about your partner, then have them answer it about themselves to see if you were right.

The questions:
- Their favourite colour
- Their favourite food
- Their favourite drink
- Their favourite season
- Their favourite thing to do with downtime
- Their favourite animal
- Their favourite place
- Their favourite music artist/group
- Their favourite film
- Their favourite item of clothing

Why?

This one is purely for a little competitive fun, it is likely some answers may surprise you. This task also creates a nice opportunity to learn more about each other and endless possibilities for ongoing discussion.

IDEA: Why not add another 5 questions each so you can make it more relevant?

future planning
Together Again

Short-Term Diary Date

Rather than waiting to be together to make plans, use this week to find time to create a short-term date plan. Get out your diaries and see where you can cross over. Once you know when you'll see each other, make a plan for a date within that time if possible.

Date ideas:
- Dinner and a movie
- Visit a city or town for the day
- Book a theatre visit or concert
- Invite friends over for a games night
- Have a BBQ
- Go to a theme park or zoo
- Have a coffee date

Why?

It can be easy to just assume our partner will be free when we will be, but by sitting and making plans ahead of time it shows we respect our partner has their own life and commitments. Having something in the diary also helps to build anticipation, and nurtures positivity.

TIP: Get dressed up and make it special, even if you're not going out!

long-distance intimacy
Steam & Bubbles

Take a Bath Together

This task may require a little planning to sync up perfectly but the idea is to have a voice or video call whilst you both shower or bathe.
Your partner's voice will soothe you as you wash the day off, or get ready for the day ahead.

Make it more:
- Use a product that your partner has picked, or their products to bring a familiar scent into the experience
- Try to pick a time when you don't have to rush and can take extra time to enjoy a little more self-care than usual
- Let conversation flow naturally, starting with simply catching up

Why?

Having company in the bathroom is quite an intimate activity, it's generally not time shared with anyone else. Having your partner with you whilst performing a little self-care will help you feel connected and together.

TIP: There are no limits here, if you are comfortable you can let the mood take it further.

8

digital dating
The 500 Mile Drive-In

Movie Night!

This weeks task is to watch a movie together. This can be done at home by syncing your streams or by visiting a local cinema to see a movie around the same time. If you go for the cinema option make sure you will have time to chat after the movie.

Make it more:
- Choose their snacks - use a delivery service to surprise order for each other
- Dress up for your date and send selfies of the getting ready process - and the getting "unready" afterwards if you want to
- Dress in something which matches the movie's theme - or go all the way and dress up as characters and rate each others efforts
- After the movie, make time to discuss your favourite characters, scenes and critique the movie together

Why?

Who doesn't love a movie night? There is no reason to miss out just because you're far away, anything is possible with a little creativity! This distance date idea is a really good way to feel connected and close with your partner whilst creating brand new discussion topics to keep you engaged.

IDEA: Can't decide on a movie? Why not pick a series to distance binge together?

9

just for fun
Just Like Me... But Far Worse

Worst Selfie Competition

As you go through your day, look for an opportunity to take the worst, most awkward or funniest selfie you can think of. You could add a theme or some rules if wanted.

Some inspiration:
- Drag in willing victims including pets, children, family or friends and see what scenario you can roleplay together
- See if a police officer or security guard is willing to pose with you
- See what interesting or awful filters you can find to "enhance" your selfie
- Use clothes belonging to your partner or children
- Paint your face or add a little makeup

Why?

This task is all about lighthearted fun; being silly together is great for your mental well-being as well as your connection with your partner. A good hit of shared dopamine makes the longer days feel far less overwhelming.

IDEA: Challenge each other to recreate selfies posted by celebrities and play "Guess Who?"!

thoughtful gifting
Getting Date Ready

Something To Look Foward To

There are no limits on this task, you simply have to choose something your partner can use, wear or take the next time you're together. Make it as simple or ambiguous as you like. You can also set a budget or theme if wanted.

Some inspiration:
- Pick an outfit, or an item of clothing to form part of (or for under) their outfit
- Choose some shoes for them to wear
- Pick a new or old favourite scent
- If you have an activity date planned, pick something practical. For example, you could buy a backpack for a hike, or a book about a place you're going to visit etc.
- If you need a budget-friendly option, create a digital itinerary and a formal invite to your next date instead

Why?

Of course the very best part of long-distance relationships is the part where the distance is closed! This task helps to build a little excitement and anticipation - no matter how soon or long it will be before your next date.

TIP: Why not plan a surprise date and buy them something useful for it, to give them a clue?

long-distance intimacy
Start Your Day With Me

A Voice Note a Day

For this task, you will send a daily voice note to your partner for a week. What your voice note contains is entirely up to you. If inspiration is in short supply, you can use the prompts below to get started.

Optional prompts:
- The thing I am looking forward most to in the next 24hrs is:
- The best part of the last 24hrs was:
- My plans for the next few hours are:
- Something I miss about you:
- Something I am looking forward to relating to us:

Why?

A voice note is a great way to slot more communication into a tight schedule, and it is so much more personal. A lot of tone, emotion and expression is lost in text messages - using the odd voice note enables love and emotion to be conveyed effectively from a distance. Of course, hearing your partner's voice should always be a positive thing too.

IDEA: Switch out the voice note for a daily video message for even more impact.

digital dating
Just You, Me & the Great Outdoors

Take a Walk Together

Plan a time when you can take a walk together whilst chatting. Share your surroundings whilst catching up.

Make it more:
- Have a competition to see who can get the most steps in over the week
- See who can take the most impressive walk location selfie
- Take walks at sunrise or sunset to see who gets the prettiest photo
- Walk somewhere you'd like to go with your partner and show them why they'd love it
- If you need to, do errands whilst you walk to make your schedules match

Why?

We can all be guilty of forgetting to appreciate the little things. Getting outside for a simple walk is so good for our mental and physical health. Having your partner join you offers a unique and intimate opportunity to connect. Time your walk to watch the sunset together to create a spiritual link.

IDEA: If you prefer, plan a long-distance gym buddy session and share your achievements.

just for fun
A Meme a Day Keeps the Distance Away

My Week in Memes

Try and find a meme, gif, photo, screenshot or article each day to be your "top thing I saw today". If you like a bit of friendly competition, at the end of each day you could decide who had the best submission. Remember there are no rules here, it can be anything you see (ideally online) that makes you laugh, happy, sad or even just something you relate to.

Some ideas:
- Pick a theme and try to outdo your partner's submission
- Search for a meme or gif using your names, home towns or hobbies to see if you can find something relatable and funny
- Try having a conversation with only memes, gifs and screenshots

Why?

Gen Z has been heard saying "True love is finding someone to tag in memes" - and believe it or not, there is some sense behind it, especially for long-distance couples. Sharing something that makes you feel gives lots of new topics to discuss and create a connection over. Of course, there is potential for learning about each other a little here too.

TIP: If you struggle, head to a website like 'Memedroid' to get inspiration.

digital dating
Escape the Distance

Online Escape Room

Find an online escape room provider, set a time and get stuck in! There are many providers online: check out some of the most popular, such as Escape Live, The Panic Room Online or Wolf Escape Games. You could pick one together or each pick a game and slot two in over the week. You'll need a pen, some paper and no distractions or interruptions to get through the game in time!

Make it more:
- Dress up for the occasion in theme with your escape room experience
- Add on a digital dinner date to make it last the night

Why?

Escape rooms have taken the world by storm recently and with good reason. One of the few things we can thank COVID for is the ability to participate in escape rooms online. For minimal cost, and often just an hour, this activity allows you to work as a team, depending on each other's skills and strengths to solve the puzzle before time is up. It's a great activity to remind you how well you work as a team and to impress your partner with your quick thinking. If you don't manage it, it will at least create lots of laughs and talking points for weeks and months to come.

IDEA: You could each invite a few friends over to play as a team or as two competing teams.

15

emotional connection
The Moments I Miss You Most

The Good, The Bad and The Ugly

Each evening, either by text or phone, tell your partner about the best and worst parts of your day. You can simply cover your best and worst moments and let the conversation flow from there, or use some/all of the prompts below to encourage sharing some connecting thoughts and observations.

Optional prompts:
- The worst thing that happened today was:
- The best part of my day was:
- The part of my day that would have been much improved if you'd been here was:
- The part of my day you'd have hated was:
- Something I learned today:
- The most dull part of my day was:

Why?

When you're living separate lives it is almost impossible to fully keep up to date with the little things we would often talk about over dinner or throughout the evening. This task is about sharing those moments to bridge the gap the distance creates to feel more connected.

IDEA: Make it more by taking a few photos throughout your day to share whilst chatting.

thoughtful gifting
The Book That Changed My Life...

Long-Distance Book Club

Pick a book that left a lasting impression and gift a copy to your partner to read. You can agree to read the same book together or to each read a different book chosen for you by your partner.

Make it more:
- Keep your partner updated with your progress so you can chat about the storyline as it progresses
- Spend a little time reading to each other over the phone - allowing your partner's voice to soothe and relax you at the end of your day
- After reading, suggest a book for your partner inspired by their choice for you

Why?

We can all be guilty of judging a book by its cover or simply reading within our comfort genres, so this activity is the gift of experience sharing. Of course, it also creates plenty of conversation starters and some unique insight regarding what makes your partner tick.

IDEA: Make it a monthly task, taking it in turns to choose books to read together.

long-distance intimacy
Barry White Time

Playlist & Chill

This task is a solo endeavour with time to compare your finished projects at the end of the week. The aim is for you to create your own playlist to suit together-time. Specifically, the playlist should be suitable to play in the background whilst you unwind together and reconnect after time apart.

Make it more:
- You could score each song on your partner's list, giving extra points for songs you have on your list too and see who gets the highest score
- Create a couple of lists for different vibes and occasions
- Create another playlist for your partner to listen to when you/they are on their way over to get you in the mood for togetherness
- Create a playlist for each genre of music you both like

Why?

Music can define your mood and shape the way you feel. Having some go-to playlists for your together time which suit the vibe and contain music you both enjoy will help you enjoy time together. It is also a great way to remind each other about your shared tastes and interests.

TIP: Try not to put any expectations on your playlist which may take the magic away.

future planning
Before We Kick The Bucket

Our Bucket List

Spend the week solo working on a relationship bucket list before sharing your lists and seeing which will stay on the shared list. If you're unsure where to start, use the below list for inspiration.

Some inspiration:
- Places you'd like to travel to together
- Activities such as extreme sports, experiences or tourism activities
- Things you'd like to learn together, such as languages, or a hobby like dancing
- Assets you'd like to have, including cars, properties, furniture, collectables, etc.
- Family goals and experiences you'd like to tick off

Why?

They say time flies when you're having fun, but the truth is time flies whether you're having fun or not. It is so important for mental well-being to enjoy life in between work, practicalities and chores. This task is about creating a list to achieve together as a couple. There is no end date so the list can be as crazy as you want it to be!

IDEA: Write two lists - one for your shared plans, and one of your own and share both.

emotional connection
The Path That Led Me To You

Share Your Story

This task is about giving your partner insight into how your past shaped you into the person they fell in love with. Be aware delving into the past may be difficult for some. You can use these prompts to start the conversation in a positive and fun way.

Optional prompts:
- The most influential person in my childhood was:
- If I could tell 10-year-old me anything, it would be:
- My earliest childhood memory is:
- The best holiday I ever went on was:
- When I was a child, I wanted to be:
- The luckiest thing that ever happened to me was:
- My favourite thing about school was:

Why?

A strong relationship remains strong because we understand each other's pasts and how they affect what we want and need in our present. Sharing your past creates intimacy and nurtures trust and closeness.

BONUS: Tell each other about a person you wish you hadn't lost or lost touch with.

20

thoughtful gifting
12 Months of Us

Relationship Calendar

Using meaningful photos, create a 12-month calendar for your partner online to order as a gift. You can use a website builder like Photobox, Printerpix, Funky Pigeon or Snapfish to put it together easily.

You can either gift immediately or save to gift in December for the year ahead. If you are not the patient type, you could design and print your own using online software or an app such as Picollage or Canva with the calendar starting the next month.

If you don't have many pictures together, create a silly calendar with month-themed selfies to make your partner laugh, or just photos you find online that you think your partner will enjoy or appreciate.

If you can edit photos before uploading, you could include a monthly love note with the image.

Why?

This task creates a year's worth of discussion and bonding opportunities, as well as a visual reminder of your love for your partner. At the end of the week, you'll have each created a gift which required care, time, effort and thought - all things which will help your partner feel loved, secure and valued. It's the perfect relationship-strengthening task!

IDEA: If you have many photos, you could make a collage for each months page.

future planning
Right, Move Me Now... Or Later Maybe

Pinned Properties

This task is somewhere between realistic future planning and setting out shared dreams and aspirations. The idea is that you share some properties from RightMove, or whatever your local equivalent is. You can create your own rules and themes here, but to help you on your way, we've listed some ideas below.

Some inspiration:
- My lottery-win dream property
- My realistic dream next property
- My dream second property
- My realistic retirement home
- My dream retirement home

Why?

Because this task offers a little bit of crazy, there's the potential for some shared laughs, but the important parts are showing what you want to achieve together and what it looks like. It's great because it naturally opens a conversation that can be big and overwhelming for those living the long-distance life. This task is a great way to communicate your end goals for your relationship light-heartedly.

TIP: This task would be fun to repeat annually to show you how much your lives change over time.

closing the distance
Real Snail Mail

Send a Postcard

This one is exactly what it says on the tin! It may require a little time to go out to find somewhere that stocks postcards as they are not as common as they used to be. Most places will stock them around tourist attractions and information centres. Once you have found one, be sure to write a nice message on the back. There is a little excitement to be had as postcards are far from confidential, so why not write a little message that only your partner will understand, or look online for a secret code generator, write in code and keep the key handy to decipher your partner's postcard when you receive it.
If you can't make it work, use something like Funky Pigeon to design a postcard for direct delivery.

Why?

In a world of digital communication, we don't feel the magic of having physical communication that generations before us depended on so heavily. Having something arrive on the doormat is fun and exciting, and of course there's the added anticipation as you await delivery - all healthy and positive emotions in a long-distance relationship. Your postcards can then be displayed somewhere as a physical reminder of your love, with the message safely hidden from view.

TIP: If you struggle to find a postcard, try an art gallery or museum gift shop.

the challenge cup
Picture Post-Its

Forehead Pictionary

For this task, you'll need a little time where you are both free for a video call and a pack of Post-it notes (or some paper and decorator's tape). On your turn, stick the paper or Post-it on your forehead, and try to draw an object for your partner to guess.

If wanted, you can set a limit on the amount of guesses your partner may make, or limit the amount of time before you move on to the next go.

As this one is tricky, it may help to set a theme such as animals, household items, activities, etc.

You can also use websites like wordrawapp.com to generate ideas before you take your turn.

Why?

Laughing together is one of the best things you can do for your relationship, and this game will definitely bring some big laughs! Combined with the light-hearted silliness, tasks like this which create some friendly competition are a great way to make memories together and maintain rapport.

IDEA: Have an extra point system based on the quality of the finished drawing

24

just for fun
7 Context-Free Days

Worst Photographer Challenge

Look for opportunities to take photos which are ambiguous in nature. The photos should be sent without any context or explanations, leaving your partner to guess what the subjects in the photos are. At the end of the week, you should decide who was the most successful and creative and they should be crowned the champion!

Some inspiration:
- A close-up body part on a monument or statue
- A cropped photo of packaging or a label which is offensive or funny when cropped
- Something you have seen outside which is unpleasant
- Pictures of things out of place

Why?

One of the best things you can do to strengthen your relationship from a distance is to invite your partner into your world and share what you're experiencing – but what if we told you we could turn that into a game that will have you both giggling at your phones like you did in the beginning? This task will bring fun to your entire day as you look for photo opportunities to outdo your partner's efforts, making you feel connected even in the most distant moments.

TIP: Don't forget to take a zoomed out photo so that you can add the context later.

25

digital dating
Couples Who Play Together Stay Together

Gaming Buddies

Find a game or app you will both enjoy and have a daily competition to get the best score. If you're not normally into games and are unsure where to start, see the list below for inspiration, but there really doesn't need to be any rules about what you choose, as long as there is a scoring system you can use to compete.

Some ideas:
- Duolingo - learn a language together and try to beat each other's high score
- Wordle - compete with this quick daily quiz
- Gidd.io - this online gaming platform offers many different games and private "rooms" to play in
- RPGs where you create an avatar, enabling you to interact and complete quests together digitally

Why?

This task uses games, puzzles and learning together to connect you. Not only will it bring a little friendly competition to your communication but it is also a great way to add some fun and diversity to your week. Relationship-wise, you'll be able to bond over skills and learning styles whilst enjoying some downtime together.

TIP: Not into games? Compete to finish the daily crossword in the paper instead.

emotional connection
7 Ways To Say I Love You

Partner Text Quiz

Answer a question a day, via text or call, or set aside time to go through all questions together.

The questions:
- What is their most attractive feature?
- What you are most proud of them for?
- What about them motivates you to be better?
- What positive change has being with them brought for you?
- How do you describe them when someone asks what they are like?
- What is the thing you're looking most forward to when you're next together?
- What do you think your partner will achieve over the next year?

Why?
There are so many different ways to tell someone how you feel about them and whilst "I love you" is MEANT to trump them all, when all you have is your words, getting more creative with them can go a long way. This task focuses on what you love about your partner, enabling them to feel loved and secure, strengthening your bond.

BONUS: Come up with your own question(s) for each other to answer.

the challenge cup
The Great Distance Bake-Off

The Golden Apron Challenge

Set up a Great Distance Bake-Off challenge where you choose a category or specific recipe and have to out-bake each other from a distance. Do the taste test on a video call and rate each other's bakes on presentation, composition, creativity, success and facial expressions through the all-important taste test.

Make it more:
- Invite a third-party judging panel to score your bakes for you
- Have friends take part with you
- Do an epic three-course bake-off
- Bake cakes to package up (very carefully) and send a slice to each other
- Choose something freezer-friendly so you can take some back for your partner the next time you are together

Why?

Challenges like this create great opportunities for week-long banter, light-hearted fighting talk and lots of laughs. This task enables you to sync up, connecting the space between you - it's also a great way to wind down and take yourself away from the everyday without much effort or expense.

TIP: Keep it manageable! If you choose a theme that is too complex you may take the fun away.

just for fun
I Did Not Predict That!

Predicted Text Time

Ever wondered what your phone thinks about you? It's time to find out in this hilarious predictive text challenge. Starting with each of the following prompts, tap the first word suggested by your phone's predictive text function and keep going until you find a natural stopping point.

Start points:
- I am sorry that I...
- I wish I could...
- I love you because...
- I really miss...
- Do you think we should...
- We should get...
- Today was...

Why?

This one is just for the laughs. You'll find the suggestions from your phone contain a lot of the things you often say to each other or often talk about, but always completely out of context. You may even find something within your output message becomes a long-standing joke or inspires a new nickname.

IDEA: Pick your own starting statement to get some more relevant endings.

29

future planning
Take Me Away

Our Next Holiday!

This is exactly what it says on the tin – it's time to talk about your next holiday together! Whether it's affordable now or not, you can start the conversation and get ready for when the time is right. If you need a little help getting started, you can use the prompts below.

Some inspiration:
- Consider your budget and timeline to save
- Consider how much time you can each take away from your commitments and when you'll be able to fit it into your schedules
- Talk about who you'll take with you
- Think about where you'd like to go and what you'd like to do there
- Decide if it will be active, relaxed or a mix of both

Why?

Whilst in a long-distance relationship it can be easy to fall into a habit of only ever planning your next visit without ever looking further ahead. Even if you're not in a position to book a holiday right away, it's nice to have ideas and a timeline to work towards and to look forward to together This task is designed to help you do exactly that.

TIP: If finance or time is tricky, plan a day out with long walks and a yummy picnic instead.

long-distance intimacy
When We're Next Together

My Bed Bucket List

This task is an opportunity to tell your partner anything you'd like to explore within your sexual relationship. This could be something as simple as wanting to show your partner some nice nightwear you bought, or something that is a much deeper fantasy.

Whilst discussing, be sure to stay within each other's boundaries and to introduce new ideas gently, without pressure or urgency.

Some ideas:
- Are there zones on your body you like to be touched that your partner doesn't know about?
- Is there something that gets you in the mood?
- Is there something your partner only did once that you really loved?
- Is there an item or outfit you'd like to introduce or try?

Why?

In a long-distance relationship, the build-up to intimacy can sometimes feel rushed and pressured given that opportunities are scarce. Having safe conversations which start foreplay early can not only facilitate better sex but also increase trust which in turn improves both desire and drive.

TIP: Remember, there's a time and place for intimate talk - get consent before starting!

31

digital dating
Relaxation Date

Home Spa Experience

This one requires a little prep work as you both need to do a little shopping ahead of your spa date. You can either each pick your own products, choose together and sync up, or order for each other.
Once you have all your items, find a time to use them whilst on a call.

Some ideas:
- Face masks
- Foot treatment socks
- Hair masks
- Aromatherapy candles
- Exfoliating scrubs/mitts
- Cuticle and nail oils
- Eye masks
- Deep moisturising treatments

Why?

There's a lot to be said for what self-care does for our mental well-being and emotional resilience - and both are key to maintaining a happy and healthy long-distance relationship. When performing self-care together, you create quiet moments for connection, reflection, recharging and appreciating each other that strengthen your bond.

TIP: If you don't know where to start, search online for a premade home spa set.

the challenge cup
Legs Eleven

Long-Distance Bingo

Make your own bingo cards and find an online bingo caller or random number generator for a good, old-fashioned game of bingo! You can choose prizes for lines and full houses and play a long session or a quick daily game.

Prize Ideas:
- Cash - although this will work best if you invite friends too so the kitty is a little more impressive
- The winner chooses the plans for your next date
- The winner gets to choose what their partner has them saved under in their phone for a week
- The winner chooses their partner's phone lock screen for a week

Why?

Sometimes it is the simple things that bring the most joy. Bingo is a much-loved game that has stood the test of time for a reason, and it works just fine long-distance. It also works well with friends, creating a nice social opportunity with no travelling required.

IDEA: If you want higher stakes, join an online game of bingo together. **Gamble responsibly.**

33

thoughtful gifting
Wearing Your Heart On Your Sleeve

Matching Jewellery

Find a budget-friendly item your partner can wear daily to remind them of you and act as a physical reminder of your relationship.

Some ideas:
- A watch - potentially engraved, or a smartwatch to enable you to track steps together
- Matching bracelets, or choose a charm to attach to existing jewellery
- Necklaces with matching charms
- Earrings or body jewellery - depending on piercings
- Pick an item of everyday clothing for each other
- If the budget allows, search "Long Distance Bracelets" to see touch-sensitive Bluetooth jewellery. These bracelets send notifications whenever touched by your partner.

Why?

Buying a simple gift to be worn daily when apart works as a brilliant visual and physical reminder of our partner and can help give strength in the quiet or difficult moments the distance creates.

IDEA: If jewellery isn't for you, print a photo with a message written on for their purse/wallet.

emotional connection
··
The Fact of the Matter is...

Every Day is a School Day!

Set out to share a fact with your partner each day. Ideally, it should be a fact you already knew – think about your interests, hobbies, career etc.
If you run out of ideas, you can use the below 7 daily prompts.

Optional prompts:
- Who can find the weirdest fact about an animal?
- What is the strangest Guinness world record you can find?
- What is the origin of your name?
- What is the most bizarre news story you can find?
- Who can find the best photo taken in space?
- Who can find the strangest statistic?
- Who can find the place with the funniest name?

Why?

Compatibility isn't about being the same - we all have plenty to learn from each other and it's good to be reminded that we bring different things to our relationships. This task may even bring up a new topic or interest you didn't realise you had in common!

IDEA: Find a topic you wish you understood as well as your partner does and discuss.

35

digital dating
Me, You & Whatever You Want To Do

Our Little Night In

This is probably the most basic and simple date night you will ever have! Pick a night where it works to chat whilst you do whatever you need to, and just be there for each other whilst you do it.

It might end up with one folding laundry whilst the other is finishing off a work project, and there may be minutes at a time where no one speaks – but this is the aim. The aim is to keep each other company whilst you do whatever it is you need to do, exactly as you would if you were together.

Why?

Having a more extended period of communication, as is offered with this task, often brings out more intimate details and feelings about our days and life generally. This task also reminds you that your worlds don't need to stop for you to have time for each other.

TIP: Turn it into a video chat if you're comfortable, to make yourselves feel more together.

long-distance intimacy
The Times It Got Hot

My Top 5 Nights With You

This task is about creating a little anticipation for the future by looking back on some of the moments where you were at your closest and most compatible.

In this task, each of you should create a ranked list of your top 5 intimate memories with your partner.

Once you have your lists put together, take it in turns to share your memories, starting from the 5th and working up to the top, elaborating on the details and the reasons it made the list.

You may even find you have similar lists!

Why?

Tasks which make you think of real moments, rather than maybes and wishes, are really useful in keeping the fire alight in your relationship when you can't be together. It works well for shy partners as they don't have to talk about wants or desires, having only to say enough for their partner to identify the memory and within seconds, you're on the same page, enjoying the same thought.

TIP: Remember, there's a time and place for intimate talk - get consent before starting!

closing the distance
Happy Hamper

Wine & Cheese Tasting

There are a number of websites that offer taster hampers for long-distance wine and cheese tasting evenings! Simply find one that works with your location and budget and order in time for a date night with a difference!

For UK-based bundles, try Mouse & Grape, Chuckling Cheese Co, Cheshire Cheese Co, Hay Hampers or ask at local businesses - you'd be surprised how many can facilitate this activity.

Of course, if cheese and wine are not your jam, you can choose something that better suits your palette - but the idea is that you're both tasting the same products at the same time.

Why?

This somewhat luxurious task is a great way to make you feel like you're in the same space. You can make the task last over an evening as a digital date, or spread the tasting over a week to create daily discussion points. It's a fun and quirky way to close the distance.

IDEA: Choose and buy your own products for each other to share your favourites.

the challenge cup
You're Pretty Handy

Create Your Partner as a Hand

This task can be done together, or at leisure through the week with the photographic evidence provided at the same time.

The challenge is to use your best art skills along with anything you have lying around to dress up, decorate and change your hand to make the best likeness to your partner.

Other ideas:
- Add a timer to the challenge
- Add rules about what can and can't be used to create your masterpiece
- Bring in a third-party judge or panel to score the final pieces
- Choose your dominant hand as the canvas

Why?

This one is all about getting you laughing together, but if one of you is creative it may be an opportunity to show off some skills your partner didn't know you had. You'll certainly have a chance to show off your resourcefulness and how you cope under pressure which may be useful for future projects!

IDEA: Why not double up and do both hands, one of each of you, for double the fun!

emotional connection
Sweet Dreams

Fall Asleep Together

This one is about connecting at the end of your day. As you get ready for bed, or once you are ready, start a video or voice call with your partner to catch up on your day briefly before heading to bed.

Keep the phone connected as you drop off to sleep so you can have the quiet together time you'd have if you were in the same place.

Make it more:
- Sleep with an item of their clothing with their scent on to trick your brain into thinking they're with you
- Don't forget to tell each other what you miss most about nights together before you fall asleep

Why?

One of the most connecting times of your day is going to bed with your partner, not just for the closeness but for the quiet, peaceful space you share in these moments. Whilst you can't quite replicate that from a distance completely, this task will help to recreate the quiet intimacy and closeness.

TIP: Don't allow this to keep you awake – if sleep noise becomes disturbing, end the call.

40

just for fun
Happily Ever After

Write a Story Together

The aim of the game is to write a story together by alternating authors. Each of you writes a sentence or paragraph before handing over to the other to write the next. You can set up a group chat just for your story submissions - enabling you to read back later.
The end result should be a completely wild and unpredictable story, creating lots of laughs and fun.

Make it more:
- Once you've written your story, take it in turns to illustrate parts of it
- Put the story and images together and use an online printing service (or a home printer) to self-publish a copy for you to keep
- If you are struggling with inspiration, choose a friend or two each to join in which will take things in a completely different direction

Why?

This light-hearted task keeps fun at the centre of your relationship and will create lots of laughs you'll connect over for a long time after the cover is closed. It also has the potential to create a fun and unique keepsake which will be treasured for years to come.

TIP: You can use an online tool to host your story like TaleAStory.co or Solentro.co.uk if wanted.

closing the distance
Have you heard?

Weirdest News Day

Try to find a news story from each day relating to the place you currently are which is shocking in some kind of way. Submit your news articles to each other either daily or all at once at the end of the week and score each chosen article on whatever measures you think it deserves recognition for.

At the end of the week, add up the points and see who gets the crown for being in the kookiest place!

Set your own boundary lines, themes and rules to make it trickier if wanted.

Why?

This task is half about connecting the space between you and helping you to relate to each other's locations, whilst equally creating fun and interesting topics to keep you connected emotionally. This kind of task helps most when you're finding the distance particularly difficult as laughing together is always the best remedy.

IDEA: Add extra points for whoever finds the best serious faces on their press photos.

digital dating
··
Wish You Were Here

My Favourite Place

Plan a trip to your favourite place and give your partner a virtual tour. This can be done in 3 different ways, detailed below.

Options:
- Record videos as you explore, with narration, to send to your partner later
- Take photographs as you explore to show your partner later whilst on the phone so you can talk about them as you look together
- Arrange a time that works for you to give a live video tour to your partner from your favourite place

Why?

This task gives your partner some exclusive insight into your brain by showing them one of your happy places. It also closes the distance by bringing your partner into your world and connecting the space between you. This task also could end with plans to visit again together, creating anticipation for a date idea you otherwise wouldn't have planned.

IDEA: Let your partner choose a place they'd love to visit and host a second tour there.

future planning
The Places We'll Go, The Things We'll See...

Our 5 Year Plan

This week is all about mapping out your future together. It's a great way of opening the conversation regarding how you both see your relationship growing over the next 5 years when approached openly and sensitively! If you're unsure how to start the conversation try the prompts.

Optional prompts:
In the next 1, 3 and 5 years, what do you see for:
- Your career and commitments
- Your family obligations & plans
- Your holidays (a great time to discuss booking!)
- Your child and pet situation
- Your living situation
- Your financial situation
- Our relationship

Why?

This one is a heavy one, so if you're having a rough week, try another number and come back at a time your bond is at its strongest. When brought up in a positive healthy space, this task will remind you both what you're working for and remind you to stay positive!

TIP: Remember the aim is to learn from each other, you don't need to fully align!

44

just for fun
Monkey Hear, Monkey Do

Reverse Charades

Just like ordinary charades, you take turns to act out an answer until your partner guesses correctly, however, this is charades with a twist - see the game below.

How to play:
- On your turn, choose a film, book or phrase to have your partner guess - however, as your partner can't see you, you'll be describing to them what they need to do so they can act out your answer, without telling them what it is
- Continue to instruct until they get the answer right
- If you like working under pressure, add a 3-minute timer per turn
- Go for the best of 3 games, or 5, or even 9
- Turn it into a week-long tournament if wanted

Why?

We can often fall into a routine of simply hopping from one responsibility to the next, never stopping to just enjoy the moment. This is particularly hard to overcome in a long-distance relationship. This game is the perfect answer to those challenges and a great way to bond and be silly together.

TIP: Need inspiration? Visit this website: www.getcharadesideas.com

thoughtful gifting
You Time, On Me!

Plan an Experience

Book a surprise activity for your partner to enjoy a little relaxation or fun in your absence. If you need some inspiration to decide what you should book, use the ideas below.

Some ideas:
- Book a massage, facial or other spa treatment
- Book an afternoon tea or bottomless brunch
- Book an experience like driving a sports car, or going in an air balloon or helicopter
- Book a pre-paid hair, nail or beauty appointment
- Book tickets to go and see an exhibition, museum or attraction they would enjoy
- Book transport for a day in a city they love visiting or that they'd like to visit
- Book tickets to an event such as the theatre or a concert

Why?

If you can't get quality time together, the least you can do is get some quality me-time to look after yourselves. Taking enough space to relax and unwind means your time together will be more relaxing and focused. It also shows love and care, fostering relationship security.

TIP: Be sure you are clear about each other's availability before booking!

long-distance intimacy
For Your Eyes Only

Private Photoshoot

This week, your task is to take at least one photo that is for your partners eyes only.

This can be fully clothed, in an outfit they love to see you in, or in whatever outfit (or lack thereof) wanted, but it must be only for each others eyes.

Make the effort to perform your self-care before your photoshoot as if you were going on a first date with your partner, and take a snap you know they'll love and cherish.

There must be no expectations or pressure surrounding this task to go beyond your own comfort zone. Always be safe and be aware that photos sent can fall into the wrong hands unexpectedly.

Why?

This task creates a little lust and love in preparation for your next date. Whether your photo shows your date-night outfit or what you might wear underneath, it's the perfect way to keep you both focused on together time. When you are together again, if the vibe is right, you could recreate your photo for your partner, that way, any future photos will carry even more anticipation.

TIP: Ask for consent before sharing your photo to prevent it being opened in company.

47

thoughtful gifting
Things That Make Me Think About You...

The Giftbag Challenge

Use either an online grocery website or a local delivery service to buy your partner a bag of treats and things that make you think of them. Set a budget or theme if wanted. This task works best when scheduled for downtime to enjoy the contents.

Some inspiration:
- What is their favourite sweet treat?
- What do they reach for when stressed?
- Can you add flowers, a nice candle or personal care products?
- What is their favourite drink?
- What have you tried recently that you think they would like?
- What is something you always have together?
- OR go for a bag with something to eat, drink, do, read and use.

Why?

Every relationship has its shared favourites when it comes to shopping for the mundane. This challenge allows you to remind your partner of together-time by sending them a little parcel full of love and thought on whatever budget you choose.

IDEA: If you want to make it trickier, you can set a colour or theme for all items within the bag.

future planning
Healthy Prospects

Our Health Goals

Use this week to discuss what health goals you each have for yourselves. This can be eating more fruit, having less sugar, going to the gym more or getting in more steps. It's about supporting each other to achieve long-term health goals.

Avoid setting weight goals unless you're already on a weight loss/gain journey as this can force us to look in the wrong places to measure success and it is not the object of the task.

See if you can find joint goals which you can work together on.

If you already have your desired fitness and health, set a goal for something you want to do or achieve such as taking part in an event or experience which you can work up to.

Why?

This task is about encouraging each other to be the best versions of ourselves. Our partner should be our greatest supporter, and creating opportunities to show that strengthens your bond.

TIP: This task is about supporting our partners goals, not setting goals for them.

closing the distance
Life Support Line

Help Out With a Practical Task

Got an appointment you need to make? Or a task in the house you hate doing but is becoming ever more urgent? This is the week to support each other in achieving the previously unachieved.

Each of you can list up to a task a day - or a big task which has a deadline of the end of the week which is sitting heavy on your to-do list. Depending on the task, you can either set aside a time you're both available so you can chat whilst your partner gets their task done, or if viable, you can swap out items from each other's lists to do for each other.

Why?

Life is overwhelming at the best of times, but in a long-distance relationship it can feel even harder due to navigating the everyday mostly alone. This task is all about helping each other to not feel so lonely in the day-to-day stuff and helps to show you both that you can be there for each other, no matter the distance.

TIP: Don't forget to review all you've achieved at the end of the week!

50

just for fun
A Ditty or Two

Write a Poem

Write a poem (or a song) for your partner. It can be as long or short as you like, and it doesn't need to rhyme! Try to make it lighthearted to make it fun to share. There are lots of free, helpful tools online if writing is not your thing, see the list below.

Useful resources:
- Grammarly - a tool which helps with spelling and grammar
- Thesaurus.com - a great website to help you find synonyms
- Poem-Generator.org.uk - a website which uses your ideas and creates a poem for you
- Various AI tools - tell an AI site what you want to create and it will do the hard work for you

Why?

Writing a poem, with or without help, is a labour-intensive task. This makes it a perfect way to make your partner feel loved, secure and valued. With the potential for lots of laughs too, this task is perfect for connecting with your partner and keeping the romance alive.

TIP: There are endless guides online to help you write your poem - just search 'write a poem'.

long-distance intimacy
When We're Apart...

The Things I Miss Most

Tell your partner what physical touch you miss the most when you are apart, whether that's something simple like a neck or foot massage or something which forms part of sexual foreplay. Likewise, tell your partner what you miss in terms of being able to touch them. Your approach here depends on your relationship, you can either choose to stay within safe and comfortable boundaries, or use this task as an excuse to be a little more flirty.

Remember, intimate conversations should be had when mutually agreeable to prevent any inappropriate notifications at inconvenient moments which will ruin any potential connection and intimacy.

Why?

When you're unable to be intimate with your partner it can really affect all aspects of your relationship. Having little intimate chats keeps that fire alive whilst building anticipation for your next meet!

TIP: Agree a code word with your partner you can use to ask for consent to send intimate texts.

Indexes

INDEX BY CATEGORY

THOUGHTFUL GIFTING

- ☐ 1. OUR STORY IN PHOTOS
- ☐ 17. THE BOOK THAT CHANGED MY LIFE...
- ☐ 21. 12 MONTHS OF US
- ☐ 34. WEAR YOUR HEART ON YOUR SLEEVE
- ☐ 46. YOU TIME, ON ME!
- ☐ 48. THINGS THAT MAKE ME THINK ABOUT YOU...
- ☐ 11. GETTING DATE READY

CLOSING THE DISTANCE

- ☐ 3. SONGS I SING ABOUT YOU
- ☐ 23. REAL SNAIL MAIL
- ☐ 38. HAPPY HAMPER
- ☐ 42. HAVE YOU HEARD?
- ☐ 50. LIFE SUPPORT LINE

EMOTIONAL CONNECTION

- ☐ 2. 7 DAYS OF US
- ☐ 16. THE MOMENTS I MISS YOU MOST
- ☐ 20. THE PATH THAT LED ME TO YOU
- ☐ 27. 7 WAYS TO SAY I LOVE YOU
- ☐ 35. THE FACT OF THE MATTER IS...

DIGITAL DATING

- ☐ 4. DINNER FOR 1 + 1
- ☐ 9. THE 500 MILE DRIVE-IN
- ☐ 13. JUST YOU, ME & THE GREAT OUTDOORS
- ☐ 15. ESCAPE THE DISTANCE
- ☐ 26. COUPLES WHO PLAY TOGETHER...
- ☐ 32. RELAXATION DATE
- ☐ 36. ME, YOU & WHATEVER YOU WANT TO DO
- ☐ 43. WISH YOU WERE HERE

INDEX BY CATEGORY

JUST FOR FUN

- [ ] 5. IT'S SO UNFUNNY, I CAN'T STOP LAUGHING
- [ ] 10. JUST LIKE ME... BUT FAR WORSE
- [ ] 14. WHAT DO YOU MEME?
- [ ] 25. 7 CONTEXT-FREE DAYS
- [ ] 29. I DID NOT PREDICT THAT!
- [ ] 41. HAPPILY EVER AFTER
- [ ] 45. MONKEY HEAR, MONKEY DO
- [ ] 51. A DITTY OR TWO

FUTURE PLANNING

- [ ] 7. TOGETHER AGAIN
- [ ] 19. BEFORE WE KICK THE BUCKET
- [ ] 22. RIGHT, MOVE ME NOW... OR LATER MAYBE
- [ ] 30. TAKE ME AWAY
- [ ] 44. THE PLACES WE'LL GO, THE THINGS WE'LL SEE
- [ ] 49. HEALTHY PROSPECTS

THE CHALLENGE CUP

- [ ] 6. MINE & THEIRS
- [ ] 24. PICTURE POST-ITS
- [ ] 21. 12 MONTHS OF US
- [ ] 28. THE GREAT DISTANCE BAKE OFF
- [ ] 33. LEGS ELEVEN
- [ ] 39. YOU'RE PRETTY HANDY

LONG-DISTANCE INTIMACY

- [ ] 8. STEAM & BUBBLES
- [ ] 12. START YOUR DAY WITH ME
- [ ] 18. BARRY WHITE TIME
- [ ] 31. WHEN WE'RE NEXT TOGETHER
- [ ] 37. THE TIMES IT GOT HOT
- [ ] 47. FOR YOUR EYES ONLY
- [ ] 52. WHEN WE'RE APART...

INDEX BY SPEND

NO SPEND TASKS

2	8	14	25	33	40	47	1*
3	9	16	26	35	41	49	17*
5	10	18	27	36	42	50	21*
6	12	19	28	37	44	51	24*
7	13	20	31	39	45	52	30*
							43*

*can be done with no spend but may require minor adjustments

BUDGET-FRIENDLY TASKS

1	11	17	23	32	48	24*	43*
9	15	21	29	34		30*	

*can be done in a budget-friendly way but may require minor adjustments

BIGGER BUDGET TASKS

29	34	46		1*	15*	32*
30	38			11*	17*	

*can be done in a budget-friendly way but may require minor adjustments

INDEX BY TASK STYLE

DAILY MINI TASK

2	7	13	20	27	36	42	50
4	8	14	22	28	37	44	52
5	10	16	25	31	40	45	
6	12	14	26	35	41	49	

ONE WEEKLY TASK

1	8	17	23	29	35	41	47
2	9	18	24	30	36	42	48
3	11	19	25	31	37	43	49
4	13	20	26	32	38	44	50
5	14	21	27	33	39	45	51
6	15	22	28	34	40	46	52
7	16						

DO IT EITHER WAY

2	7	16	25	31	40	45	
4	8	17	26	35	41	49	
5	13	20	27	36	42	50	
6	14	22	28	37	44	52	

INDEX BY TIME REQUIRED

TASK TAKES LESS THAN 1HR

2	11	23	31	40	49		1*
4	12	24	33	41	50		3*
5	14	25	35	42	52		8*
6	16	26	36	45			
7	18	27	37	47			
10	20	28	39	48			

*can be in an hour but may require minor adjustments

TASK TAKES 1-3HRS

1	19	38	46		3*	26*	1-
9	21	43	51		8*	33*	26-
15	22	44			11*	36*	30-
17	29	45					

*can be adapted to fit available time

-may take 3+ hours

SAME TIMEZONE NEEDED

4   8

INDEX BY TASK STYLE

SPONTANEOUS TASKS

2	10	19	28	38	45		8*
3	12	20	31	40	49		24*
5	14	22	35	41	50		26*
6	16	25	36	42	52		
7	18	27	37	44			

*can be adapted to be done spontaneously

PLANNING REQUIRED TASKS

1	11	17	29	33	39	46	48
4	13	21	30	34	43	47	51
9	15	23	32				

About The Author

This book is the first self-published by Hannah Smart, via Amazon KDP in July 2024. Hannah has been a keen writer all her life and this book is part one of her lifelong dream to be a published author. This book was written from her personal experience in her own long-distance relationship.

A Note From The Author

Thank you so much for purchasing and reading this book - I sincerely hope that not only do you enjoy every single page, but that it gives you strength, patience and security within your relationship until you meet again.

"True love laughs
in the face of distance"

If you love this book..

Your review makes a HUGE difference, please take the time to leave one wherever you purchased from!

Want a FREE PDF/printable copy to send to your partner?

Send us a message on TikTok, or Facebook with proof of a review and we will send it over to you.

Don't forget to tag me in your TikToks - **@hannah.smart.auth**

COMING SOON (SEPT/OCT 2024)

Close the Distance - The Journal

A couples activity book to be passed between you, packed fill of amazing templates, games and tips to keep your love alive. Coming to Amazon & TikTok Shop very soon!

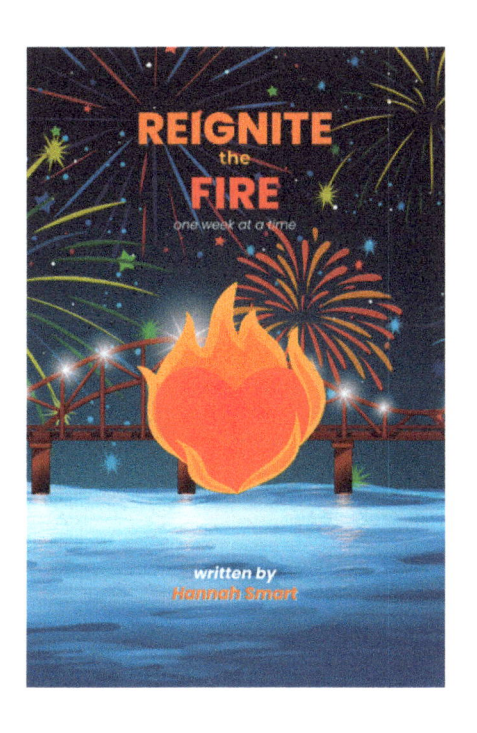

Reignite the Fire

I have now released a year-long activity book for busy couples.

Almost all tasks can be done for free from your living room. So whether you want the adapted version for when you DO close the distance or you think you have friends who will love it, check it out on Amazon now!

It has been designed to suit young parents with a tight budget and limited time, but is as inclusive and accessible as close the distance, so anyone can use it.

ART
Credit to: Olya Litvinova

Made in United States
Orlando, FL
11 September 2024